Prairie Dogs

NorthWord Press
Chanhassen, Minnesota

In honor of prairie dogs, that my great-grandchildren might hear their chirps echoing over the prairies.

Special thanks to Dr. Con Slobodochikoff, Professor of Biology at Northern Arizona University and the foremost researcher in the area of prairie dog language, and David Crawford, Executive Director of Rocky Mountain Animal Defense.

—M.L.

© NorthWord Press, 2004

Photography © 2004: Dennis K. Olivero: cover, pp. 6-7, 21, 29; Paul and Joyce Berquist: pp. 4, 18, 38-39, 41; Dominique Braud: pp. 8, 14, 22, 30; C. Allan Morgan: pp. 10, 11, 12-13, 44; Donald M. Jones: p. 24; Jeff Vanuga: p. 32; Michael H. Francis: back cover, pp. 5, 16-17, 25, 26-27, 31, 35.

Illustrations by Wayne Ford
Designed by Russell S. Kuepper
Edited by Kristen McCurry
Cover image: black-tailed prairie dog (*Cynomys ludovicianus*)

NorthWord Press
18705 Lake Drive East
Chanhassen, MN 55317
1-800-328-3895
www.northwordpress.com

Library of Congress Cataloging-in-Publication Data

Lorbiecki, Marybeth.
  Prairie dogs / Marybeth Lorbiecki ; illustrations by Wayne Ford.
      p. cm. – (Our wild world series)
Includes index.
Summary: Discusses the physical characteristics, behavior, habitat, and life cycle of prairie dogs.
  ISBN 1-55971-883-8 (hc) – ISBN 1-55971-884-6 (sc)
  1. Prairie dogs–Juvenile literature. [1. Prairie dogs.] I. Ford, Wayne, ill. II. Title. III. Series.

QL737.R68L67 2004
599.36'7–dc22

                                                    2003059993

Printed in Malaysia

10 9 8 7 6 5 4 3 2 1

Our **WILD**™
WORLD
SERIES

Prairie Dogs

Marybeth Lorbiecki
Illustrations by Wayne Ford

NORTHWORD PRESS
Chanhassen, Minnesota

THE BUSIEST PLACE for wildlife on a prairie is a prairie dog town. With burrows below and mounds above, these towns are bursting with activity. Prairie dogs are jumping, digging, wrestling, yipping, grooming, cleaning, kissing, and chasing. Their high-pitched calls and chirps ring out over the grasses.

Eagles soar overhead, and coyotes patrol. They both wait to catch a prairie dog unprepared. Bison and cattle take dust baths in the dirt mounds around the town's holes. On other mounds, burrowing owls line up and watch the action. Underground, in the prairie dogs' abandoned tunnels, snakes, spiders, salamanders, box turtles, rabbits, and mice slither and scurry. Without prairie dogs, many of these animals would be without homes and food.

Prairie dogs are extremely smart. They watch everything, have excellent memories, and chat to each other about what they see.

Prairie dog towns attract many other animals. Bison, cattle, and antelope like to graze near them.

Prairie dogs may bark, yip, and snarl, but they are not dogs. They are ground squirrels. Their ears and tails are shorter than most squirrels' and their claws are longer. Even so, prairie dogs are related to the nut-grabbing neighbors found in backyards. Prairie dogs are also related to chipmunks, woodchucks, and marmots.

With small rounded heads and ears nearly hidden in fur, prairie dogs can slip into narrow holes and winding tunnels easily. From head to tail, most prairie dogs measure from 11 to 13 inches (28 to 33 cm). The tail reaches out another 3 to 4 inches (8 to 10 cm). They have short legs, but they can run up to 35 miles (56 km) per hour for short sprints.

Prairie Dog
FUNFACT:

Prairie dogs have been called "sod poodles," "barking squirrels," "prairie rats," and *petits chiens*," or little dogs. Their scientific name, *Cynomys*, means mouse-dog squirrel.

Prairie dogs rarely go more than 30 feet (less than 10 meters) from their burrows.
That is only about the length of five adult men lined up foot to head.

This black-tailed prairie dog has fattened up for winter, when food is scarce. It will lose as much as half its body weight before spring.

In the winter and spring, prairie dogs are as slender as minks. But once the grasses start sprouting, prairie dogs spend a great deal of time eating. Through the summer and fall, they grow fatter and fatter, until their roly-poly bodies ripple as they run. The prairie dogs need this extra weight. They have to live most of the winter on their fat.

Adult prairie dogs range in weight from 1.5 to 3 pounds (.7 to 1.4 kg). They range in color from golden or reddish brown to gray, with darker ears and lighter colored bellies and snouts. Some prairie dogs look black when they have been digging in soil with coal dust, but there are no truly black prairie dogs. However, there are some rare white prairie dogs.

Prairie dogs live in Mexico, the United States, and Canada, in the dry grassy areas of the western plains and Rocky Mountain foothills. There are five different kinds, or species (SPEE-sees).

 Black-tailed	Gunnison's
White-tailed	Mexican
Utah	

The prairie dogs that like the high deserts and mountain valleys have white-tipped tails. These species are the white-tailed prairie dog, the Gunnison's prairie dog, and the Utah prairie dog. Since they live in higher places with colder temperatures, they tend to hibernate, or sleep through the harsh winters.

The white-tailed prairie dog is the most common of the high-ground species. It can be found in a few mountain meadows of Colorado, Utah, Wyoming, and Montana. It is less talkative and social than its cousins.

Prairie Dog
FUNFACT:

Grazing animals, such as cattle, bison, and antelope, like to eat near prairie dog towns. The grasses and flowers have greater nutrition and likely taste better. The grazers also use the prairie dog mounds for dirt baths to get rid of pesky insects.

White-tailed prairie dogs are found in the foothills and mountain meadows of the Rockies.

Gunnison's prairie dogs do not dig as deep as some of the other species. Their tunnels are only about 3.5 feet (1 m) deep.

The Gunnison's prairie dog has a darker body and a shorter tail than most of the other prairie dogs. The Gunnison's prairie dog can be seen in the high, dry plains of the Four Corners area. This is where New Mexico, Colorado, Arizona, and Utah meet. These dogs are more like ground squirrels than other prairie dogs. They live in smaller groups and build smaller mounds.

The Utah prairie dog is the least common of all the high-ground prairie dogs. It is easy to tell from the other species because it is the smallest and has a spot of black above the eyes. It lives in just a few places in the mountain valleys of central Utah.

The prairie dog species that live on the low, dry grasslands have black-tipped tails and do not hibernate. They are the black-tailed prairie dog and the Mexican prairie dog.

The black-tailed prairie dog is the largest and most numerous of all prairie dog species. It can be found in small patches of grasslands and prairies in Canada down through the western plains of the United States to Mexico.

Prairie Dog
FUNFACT:

Prairie dogs help prairies grow. By eating weedy plants, they keep prairie grasses and flowers from being choked out. They churn up the soil when they tunnel, loosening the soil for roots, air, and water. The prairie dogs also add fertilizer with their leavings.

The Utah prairie dog is rare. It was placed on the Endangered Species List in 1973.
It is only found in five counties of southwest Utah, high in the mountains.

When looking for food, male prairie dogs wander a bit farther from the burrow than females. This black-tailed prairie dog is enjoying a sunflower.

Though the black-tailed prairie dog is the most numerous of all the species, it is not common. Once, prairie dogs were seen all across the Great Plains of North America, along with the bison. Prairie dogs used to number in the hundreds of millions. But, like the bison, they are now only found in small areas far from each other. One particular kind of black-tailed prairie dog, the Arizona prairie dog, has died out completely. It is extinct (ex-TINKD).

The Mexican prairie dog, the other species from non-mountain areas, is extremely rare. It lives in only a few places in Mexico.

Prairie dogs are named after North America's natural grasslands. These prairies are filled with many different kinds of wild grasses and flowers, which is why prairie dogs do so well there. They are mostly vegetarians, or plant eaters. They feast on shoots, seeds, stalks, and flowers. Though they are named after the prairie, these animals are not found only in prairies. The black-tailed prairie dog can sometimes live in fields or meadows of other grasses as long as they can crop the plants short with their teeth.

The dinner of choice for prairie dogs depends on the season and what plants are growing. In times of heavy snow or during drought (DROWT), when grasses die, prairie dogs dig out and nibble roots. The dogs that live in more desert-like spaces eat prickly pear and other cactus. They also gnaw (NAW) on bushes and small trees, such as sagebrush and mesquite (mes-KEET) trees. Prairie dogs, except the white-tailed species, chew up weedy plants, too, including dandelions and thistles (THISS-uls).

Prairie Dog
FUNFACT:

Scientists estimate that it takes about 429 prairie dogs to eat the amount of grass one cow eats in a day. An adult prairie dog eats about 25 pounds (11.4 kg) of grass per year.

Members of a coterie work and talk together for protection.
These four white-tailed prairie dogs stand alert and keep watch.

Prairie dogs occasionally feed on grasshoppers or other insects. They are able to pick up small things easily because they have finger-like separations to their paws, like raccoons. So they can grasp a clump of grass or pick up a beetle.

Prairie dogs have tall front teeth, like other rodents. They can tear off a bunch of tough grasses with little effort. Then the back molars start to work, grinding these plants to a pulp. Prairie dogs have 22 teeth in all.

To wash their food down, prairie dogs only have their own saliva. They don't need to drink! Their bodies make water from some foods they eat, and they swallow dew with the plants they chew in the early mornings. There is also some water in the plants and insects they eat.

Prairie dogs use their long claws for tugging up grasses and picking up food, tunneling, grooming, and defending themselves.

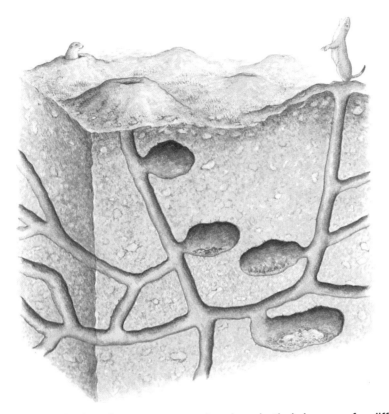

Black-tailed prairie dogs have numerous chambers in their burrows for different functions: nesting, sleeping, food storage, and others. A single tunnel can extend as far as 100 feet (about 30 m) or one-third the size of a football field.

Prairie dogs are champion diggers. They use their long claws to tunnel out group homes deep underground. The burrows of black-tailed prairie dogs usually go down at a steep slant for 12 to 15 feet (3.7 to 4.6 m). Then they flatten and spread out in long tunnels leading 20 to 50 feet (6.1 to 15.3 m) farther to escape exits. There are chambers built along the way, with rooms for storing food, birthing and nursing young, hiding, sleeping, and other uses.

In hard, dry, clay-like soils, prairie dog tunnels do not go down as deep. The digging is just too much work!

19

Prairie dogs are the most clannish members of the squirrel family. They live in large groups called coteries (KO-tir-ees). A black-tailed prairie dog coterie usually includes one adult male, three or four adult females, and their young. These coteries often live right next to other coteries, like neighborhoods in a prairie dog town. The burrows of each coterie, though, are not connected. Prairie dogs are feisty toward strangers, and they strongly defend their territories.

Prairie dogs have keen senses of smell and hearing, which help them avoid tunneling into each other's burrows. Should they do so, there would be trouble. The winner of the fight would then chase off the intruder and block the tunnel.

Prairie Dog
FUNFACT:

One prairie dog town in Texas reached 250 miles (402 km) in one direction and 100 miles (161 km) in another. It was estimated that 400 million prairie dogs lived there!

These young black-tailed pups practice being protective adults and defending their ground by rough play.

In a prairie dog town, there are usually 5 to 35 adult prairie dogs for every acre (.4 ha). A single burrow has from one to six openings. The average town ends up with more than 50 holes per acre. Not all of these are being used. Some are abandoned because predators (PRED-uh-torz) or illness killed off too many members of the coterie, or there was not enough food.

A larger town can get sectioned off into smaller parts, too. This happens if some part of the landscape splits the town, such as a river or a rocky ridge.

These young black-tailed prairie dogs are getting their first look at the outside world.

Each species of prairie dog makes the kinds of burrow entrances and exits that work best for their dirt and landscape. Black-tailed prairie dogs make three different kinds.

The first type of hole has a mound around it that looks like a little volcano. This is a major entrance, and the dogs take a great deal of time building and rebuilding the mound. They form the shape with their paws and tamp, or pack, the dirt with their foreheads. These mounds can be as tall as 3 feet (.9 m). The opening is only 6 to 12 inches (15 to 30 cm) across. It gets even narrower underground and is only 3 to 4 inches (8 to 10 cm) wide. The hole is big enough for prairie dogs, but not for coyotes!

A coterie may have more than one of these volcano mounds because they are so useful. Besides giving the dogs easy escape hatches into their homes, these volcano mounds work like watchtowers. Standing on top of the mound, the dogs get a good view in all directions of their grassy territory and the lands around it. The volcano mounds also keep rivers of rainwater from pouring down into the burrows. On hot, dry days, the mounds create an air-vent system. They draw fresh air through the tunnels to carry the heat away.

Prairie Dog
FUNFACT:

The most powerful male dog in the coterie, or the "top dog," gets the best place on the volcano mound and the first choice of grasses.

This black-tailed dog is on the run to get back to the burrow with its treasure before it gets caught!

Just underneath the opening of the volcano mound is an extra hollowed-out place big enough for a prairie dog to sit up. This is called the listening chamber. After a dog has spotted danger, such as a coyote, it will call out an alarm. Other dogs in the coterie and town will echo it and respond. The prairie dogs will all go on alert, facing the coyote, keeping their eyes on its every move.

Any dog that has strayed too far from its own holes will rush back. If it has to pop into another coterie's hole to escape the coyote, it could face danger there, too!

This time, despite these prairie dogs calling to each other, the coyote got one. Sometimes a coyote and a badger will work together to catch a dog for dinner.

If the coyote gets too close to one of the dogs on its watchtower, the dog will duck into the listening chamber to let its ears do the work. It will not pop up its head again until there is no sound of the predator or an all-clear call has been sounded by another prairie dog.

Once the coyote is seen leaving the area, one or more of the dogs watching it leave will yip the all-clear call. The other dogs will echo this. Soon all the dogs in hiding will come out and go back to their work of eating, grooming, cleaning, and mound building.

A black-tailed dog pops up from its escape hatch to see if all is safe.

The second kind of hole is a dirt hill, which is not carefully tended. It is made of all the loose dirt that came out of the tunnel when it was dug. The hills are only 4 to 5 inches (10 to 13 cm) tall, but they serve as perfect back doors.

Finally, there are escape hatches that are just holes in the ground without mounds, and sometimes without connections to tunnels. These holes are often in the sides of hills or ditches. The prairie dogs duck in them to rest, take a break from the hot summer sun, or hide.

What are the prairie dogs hiding from?

Prairie Dog
FUNFACT:

**Over 500 pounds (227 kg)
of dirt are tossed out to make
the average burrow.**

Besides coyotes, prairie dogs stay on the alert for golden eagles, red-tailed hawks, and ferruginous (feh-ROO-juh-nus) hawks flying above them. The birds can swoop down and snatch the dogs from overhead. They are so dangerous that black-tailed prairie dogs have a special alarm call just for eagles and hawks. This is a jump-yip leap backwards in the air with two fast, high-pitched notes. At that signal, everyone nearby hits the tunnels. No one waits around to watch as they do with predators on the ground.

At night, black-footed ferrets stalk the dogs. Ferrets are slim enough to travel into the burrows. They live almost entirely off of eating prairie dogs.

Badgers are also a common predator. They are such fast diggers that they can go right after a prairie dog into its tunnel. Other predators are swift foxes, weasels, bobcats, ravens, wolves, rattlesnakes, pet or stray dogs, and humans.

Prairie Dog
FUNFACT:

Besides humans, prairie dogs have the most complex language system of any animals studied by scientists. Scientists use computers to recognize the different sound bits or "words." It seems prairie dogs even have grammar rules to their language!

Scientists are fascinated by the language of prairie dogs. The dogs communicate not only to tell each other of danger, but for other reasons as well.

Prairie dogs mix actions with sounds to get attention and communicate. This jump-yip call alerts others to danger close by.

Prairie dogs protect themselves against predators by communicating with each other and working together. They are the most talkative members of the squirrel family. Their language system is amazing. Prairie dogs make many different sounds that they arrange in different ways for different messages. They also make their voices go high or low, fast or slow, and friendly or harsh to communicate different meanings.

Prairie dogs will scream when they are afraid, snarl when they fight, churr or buzz when they argue, and chirk or purr when they mate. Chirps are used to tell neighboring dogs where they are and to pass on other information. Scientists aren't sure what else is being said. Perhaps the dogs are commenting on the tastiness of certain grasses or when they should start their spring tunnel cleaning!

From far away, some of the calls

can sound like the baying of hounds. But up close, the bark of a prairie dog actually sounds more bird-like than dog-like, with a shrill *chee-chee-chee*. Each prairie dog species speaks a little differently. They have dialects (DY-a-lekts), or small differences in their calls. Gunnison's prairie dogs tend to have sharper, shorter calls than black-tailed prairie dogs. White-tailed prairie dogs are thought to have more musical tones. Even prairie dogs of the same species from different towns have slight differences in their calls.

Actions also tell a great deal. Tail flicking, jumping, bobbing, snarling, teeth chattering, and "kissing" all have meaning. When prairie dogs meet, they run up to each other, hug, and kiss. Scientists think they are actually rubbing their teeth together or checking scent glands. By taste and smell, a prairie dog can tell if another dog is a relative, friend, or enemy.

Prairie dogs greet each other by hugging and kissing. They also groom each other.

This black-tailed dog makes it clear that danger is still present.

Just like humans, prairie dogs use a combination of sounds and actions to communicate. Through careful studies and with the help of computers, scientists have discovered the meanings of some of their messages.

A jump-yip call means "Find cover!" The prairie dog closes its eyes and throws itself backward in the air while sending out a shrill "weee-oh!" sound. This urgent alarm is used by black-tailed prairie dogs to warn other dogs about eagles or hawks flying overhead, but it is not used by the species in the mountains. A bobbing bark, which has two short sounds repeated between quick bobs, means "Watch that predator." This bark often comes with a description of the predator. The all-clear whistle-like yip means "You can come out now." A snarled warning bark says "This is MY area. Stay out."

Prairie Dog
FUNFACT:

Prairie dogs describe details to each other.
They will note the difference between
colors of fur or clothing on an approaching
intruder and whether they seem dangerous.
They will even tell if a person has a gun!

These are just a few examples. The calls have individual pieces of sound that carry meaning, like words. The prairie dogs vary the words in the calls and their order to give more information. They will tell each other exactly what kind of predator is approaching, its speed, and even what it looks like, including its color and size. The dogs listening then take different actions according to which animal is on its way, from where, and how fast.

Prairie dogs also describe animals that are not a danger to them, such as antelope, deer, elk, and cows. Perhaps they do this much like newscasters give weather reports, simply to keep everyone updated on anything that might be moving, important, or surprising.

A prairie dog town is always an active place with kissing, chasing, grooming, eating, repairing mounds, cleaning out tunnels, and digging new ones. The dogs tend to rise and set with the sun. In the winter, most of the activity is underground. The high-ground prairie dogs completely hibernate during this time. The plains species simply spend less time above ground.

Prairie Dog
FUNFACT:

Prairie dogs "talk" about many things they see, even about harmless antelope and cattle that stroll by. Much of their language has yet to be decoded. Who knows what else they chat about!

Prairie dogs build up a thick fur for winter, which they shed in the spring.

When the snow covers the grasslands, prairie dogs have to dig to find food. They tend to eat far less, spending more time underground where it is warmer. They live off the fat they gained during the summer and fall.

As spring approaches, black-tailed prairie dogs start eating more and building their nests. This is a busy time. First they do some spring-cleaning, hauling out all the old, dirty grasses from the birthing chambers.

Then they drag fresh, new grasses in.

Spring is also mating time. Adult males are able to mate for only four to five weeks in spring. That's when they begin chirking their mating call, calling out their territories, and chasing any females within sight or sound.

Females are able to mate only four to five hours on a single spring day. So if they are not ready, they snarl and bite at any males that approach them.

Mother prairie dogs nurse their young for seven weeks.
They will protect the little ones against any enemies, even other prairie dog mothers.

When the females are ready to mate, they give their own chirking calls. Then every male that hears them makes a wild dash over. Sparring breaks out between the males to see who gets to mate first. Both males and females mate numerous times during this period.

After all the mating is over, the coteries settle down. The females, along with one top male, return to their home burrows. There are one to four females in each burrow. Each female has her own birthing and nursing chamber. In 34 to 35 days, the young are born. Usually, about three to five prairie dog pups are born in each chamber, but there can be as many as eight.

Dark red and wrinkled, the little pups are hairless and blind. Their eyes are shut tight. The mothers lick and rub them.

The pups are so small they fit in the palm of a child's hand. They are only 2.75 inches (7 cm) long. They weigh an average of half an ounce (14 g). That is about the weight of a few marbles.

The pups may start out tiny, but they grow fast. They drink milk from their mothers' bodies. In two weeks, they have more than doubled their size. By the fifth week, their eyes open.

However, only about half the young ever make it above ground to see sunlight. Sometimes a nursing prairie dog will attack and eat the young of another female in the burrow. It could be that the attacking mother has not had enough food to make milk and she is extremely hungry. Or she may need the other mother to help nurse her pups. Or there may not be much room to build new coteries in the area, and the attacking mother may want her pups to get the space that remains. Scientists do not know for sure what causes a mother to act this way.

Prairie Dog
FUNFACT:

Males and females mate with numerous partners. The young in any litter often have different fathers.

Young prairie dogs are called pups. They learn by watching, listening, and imitating.

Snakes, ferrets, and badgers also eat prairie dog pups. When these predators make their moves, prairie dog mothers fight to protect their pups. They will even gang up with other prairie dogs against a rattlesnake.

At six weeks old, all the pups that survive get their first look at the outside world. They play rough-and-tumble chasing games with the other pups. The adults check on the youngsters often, kissing and grooming them. When hungry, the pups come running to the closest adults to nurse. The males gently nudge them away. The females let them nurse, even if the pups are not their own young.

At seven weeks, the females also begin to nudge the pups away. Then the young must learn from the parents how to find plants and grasses to eat.

The adults have already begun teaching the pups about predators, using voice, tail, and body signals. Over the summer months, the young will begin answering back, imitating the adults.

By September, the young are almost as large as their parents, but they are not as fat or heavy. They scatter to make new homes in abandoned burrows or dig their own. Sometimes the parents will scatter instead and leave some of the young with the family burrow.

By the start of the second summer, the yearlings are about the same size as their parents. That fall, they will be fully grown. They may be ready to have young of their own the following spring, at about two years old. If food is scarce, or if other conditions are not right, they may not be ready to have young until the next spring.

Each fall and spring, the animals molt, or shed their old fur. In the spring, the new hair is thinner and shorter for the hot summer months. In the fall, it grows thicker and longer to warm them through the winter ahead.

Prairie Dog
FUNFACT:

Some of the largest prairie dog towns in the United States can be found on Native American reservations. The Cheyenne River Sioux have taken steps to protect prairie dogs and bison on their lands.

Prairie dogs in the wild live an average of four to five years. They do not grow larger with age. Some prairie dogs have been captured to live in zoos or as pets. They live an average of eight and a half years in captivity.

However, prairie dogs do not make good pets. They are great diggers, so no one's yard is safe. Also, their memories are too good! If a prairie dog feels scared or upset, or if someone mishandles a prairie dog, even by accident, the animal does not forget. It will snarl or bite or call out alarms whenever that person approaches, even if it is a month later.

In addition, captive prairie dogs can catch diseases from other animals. So even though they seem cute and friendly, it's a bad idea to capture or buy prairie dogs for pets.

This pup is looking for some attention. Both female and male adults in a coterie watch out for the young, though the females do most of the pup care.

Despite how smart and talkative prairie dogs are, their towns are shrinking and disappearing. Prairie dogs are found in less than two percent of the places they used to live. This is because most of their grassland habitats, or places for homes, have been used for ranching, farming, buildings, or roads.

Unfortunately, prairie dogs are not safe even in the national and state parks and grasslands. Government workers, ranchers, and farmers have been poisoning or shooting prairie dogs. They argue that prairie dogs eat up too much grass. They want the grass saved for cattle, sheep, and bison. They also fear that these animals will stumble in prairie dog holes and break their legs.

These are misunderstandings. Studies have shown over and over that prairie dogs do not take away important amounts of grass from cattle or sheep. The prairie dogs eat no more than four to seven percent of the grass livestock would want. Also, cattle, sheep, or horses rarely break their legs in prairie dog holes.

Prairie dogs have sometimes been feared because of disease. They are thought to carry the sickness called the bubonic plague (boo-BON-ick PLAYG). The plague is actually carried by fleas. These fleas can jump onto prairie dogs, but more often, they find a place in the fur of mice, cats, dogs, rats, rabbits, and other animals.

Prairie Dog
FUNFACT:

Prairie dogs are considered a "keystone" species. That means that many other animals depend upon prairie dogs and their towns. Scientists think the dogs are important to more than 180 other animal species.

Coyote

Golden Eagle

Badger

Swift Fox

Black-footed
Ferret

Burrowing Owl

Many species depend on prairie dogs for food and shelter.

Prairie dogs are less dangerous than many other flea carriers. When bitten by infected fleas, prairie dogs usually die within a week. As long as humans do not touch the infected prairie dogs, they will not get the disease from them.

Far from being dangerous to humans, livestock, or wildlife, prairie dogs are important to the health of all. Prairie dogs and their towns offer shelter and food to numerous other grassland species. Scientists think that about 40 species of mammals, 90 species of birds, 80 species of plants, 29 species of insects, 15 species of reptiles, and 10 species of amphibians are connected to prairie dog towns. As the numbers of prairie dogs go down, these other species struggle, too.

A Utah prairie dog looks out over its habitat. It is the smallest of all prairie dog species, with one of the smallest ranges.

The black-footed ferret is now nearly extinct in the wild. Other animals, such as the swift fox, mountain plovers, and burrowing owls, are also falling in numbers as the prairie dog numbers fall.

In 1900, prairie dog populations were thought to total about five billion in North America. Today, scientists consider all five species of prairie dogs to be either endangered (en-DANE-jurd) or threatened (THRET-end) in their survival. However, not all species are listed this way by the government. Some groups still consider prairie dogs as pests.

The future of prairie dogs lies in the hands of people. Learning about prairie dogs and telling others about them are the first steps to saving them. With greater understanding and co-operation, people can protect prairie dogs and their habitats.

By saving prairie dogs, people can also help save the many other animal species that depend upon them. For if the prairie dog goes, so do they.

Internet Sites

You can find out more interesting information about prairie dogs and lots of other wildlife by visiting these Internet sites.

www.kidsplanet.org	Defenders of Wildlife
www.desertusa.com/dec96/du_pdogs.html	Desert USA
www.enchantedlearning.com	Enchanted Learning.com
www.pup.princeton.edu/birds/mammals/dogs/dogs.html	Mammals of North America, Princeton University Press
www.nationalgeographic.com/burrow/	National Geographic
www.nwf.org/prairiedogs	National Wildlife Federation
http://pbskids.org/dragonflytv/	PBS Kids/Dragonfly TV
www.prairiedogcoalition.org	Prairie Dog Coalition
www.prairiedogs.org	Rocky Mountain Animal Defense
www.sierraclub.org/lewisandclark/species/prairiedog.asp	Sierra Club
www.nps.gov/thro/tr_dogs.htm	Theodore Roosevelt National Park
www.worldalmanacforkids.com/explore/animals/prairiedog.html	World Almanac for Kids Online

Index

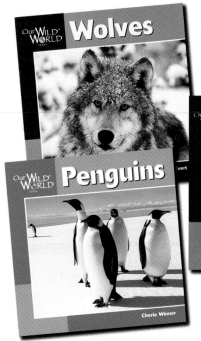

Our WILD WORLD™
SERIES

Wolves

Penguins

Lions
Cherie Winner

Sea Turtles

Manatees
Kathy Feeney